She Persisted

OPRAH WINFREY

—INSPIRED BY—

She Persisted

by Chelsea Clinton & Alexandra Boiger

• •

OPRAH WINFREY

• •

Written by
Renée Watson

Interior illustrations by
Gillian Flint

PHILOMEL

PHILOMEL BOOKS
An imprint of Penguin Random House LLC, New York

First published in the United States of America by Philomel,
an imprint of Penguin Random House LLC, 2021

Visit us online at penguinrandomhouse.com.

Library of Congress Cataloging-in-Publication Data
Names: Watson, Renée, author. | Flint, Gillian, illustrator.
Title: Oprah Winfrey / written by Renée Watson ; interior illustrations by Gillian
Flint. Description: New York : Philomel, 2021. | Series: She persisted | Includes
bibliographical references. | Audience: Ages 6–9 | Audience: Grades 2–3 | Summary:
"A biography of Oprah Winfrey, part of the She Persisted chapter book series"—
Provided by publisher. Identifiers: LCCN 2021029313 (print) | LCCN 2021029314
(ebook) | ISBN 9780593115985 (hardcover) | ISBN 9780593115992 (trade paperback)
| ISBN 9780593116005 (ebk) Subjects: LCSH: Winfrey, Oprah—Juvenile literature.
| Women television personalities—United States—Biography—Juvenile literature. |
African American television personalities—Biography—Juvenile literature. | African
American actresses—Biography—Juvenile literature. | African American women—
Biography—Juvenile literature. Classification: LCC PN1992.4.W56 W38 2021 (print)
| LCC PN1992.4.W56 (ebook) | DDC 791.4502/8092 [B]—dc23
LC record available at https://lccn.loc.gov/2021029313
LC ebook record available at https://lccn.loc.gov/2021029314

Printed in the United States of America

HC ISBN 9780593115985
10 9 8 7 6 5 4 3 2 1
PB ISBN 9780593115992
10 9 8 7 6 5 4 3 2 1

WOR

Edited by Jill Santopolo.
Design by Ellice M. Lee.
Text set in LTC Kennerley.

For
Domonique Debnam

She
Persisted

....

DEAR READER,

As Sally Ride and Marian Wright Edelman both powerfully said, "You can't be what you can't see." When Sally Ride said that, she meant that it was hard to dream of being an astronaut, like she was, or a doctor or an athlete or anything at all if you didn't see someone like you who already had lived that dream. She especially was talking about seeing women in jobs that historically were held by men.

I wrote the first *She Persisted* and the books that came after it because I wanted young girls—and children of all genders—to see women who worked hard to live their dreams. And I wanted all of us to see examples of persistence in the face of different challenges to help inspire us in our own lives.

I'm so thrilled now to partner with a sisterhood of writers to bring longer, more in-depth versions of these stories of women's persistence and achievement to readers. I hope you enjoy these chapter books as much as I do and find them inspiring and empowering.

And remember: If anyone ever tells you no, if anyone ever says your voice isn't important or your dreams are too big, remember these women. They persisted and so should you.

Warmly,

Chelsea Clinton

OPRAH WINFREY

TABLE OF CONTENTS

....

....

Every Person Is Born with Talent

Oprah Winfrey always loved telling stories. When she was a young girl, she didn't have a lot of money or a lot of fancy clothes, but she had her voice and she used her voice in big and small ways.

Oprah used her voice to tell stories to anyone—and anything—that would listen. Especially to the animals on the farm in her small Mississippi town. Oprah considered the chickens and piglets her

friends. She named each one and told them stories
as she fed them. Sometimes, she made up grand
tales. Other times, she retold the sermons she
heard at church. Oprah was good at remembering
what the pastor said on Sunday mornings, and she

was good at memorizing the scriptures her grand-mother taught her.

By the age of three, Oprah was able to read. She loved reading and speaking words, and people all around town loved hearing her. No one knew that one day she would be called the "Queen of Talk." No one knew that one day, her voice would be heard all over the world.

Oprah was born in Kosciusko, Mississippi, on January 29, 1954. Her parents were not married. Her mother, Vernita Lee, was eighteen years old. Her father, Vernon Winfrey, was away serving in the United States Army. They named her Orpah, after a woman in the Bible. People often mispronounced her name, switching the r and the p, so instead of correcting them, she took on the name Oprah.

Vernita wanted to create a better life for her

daughter. She did not want to raise Oprah in the segregated South, where Black people did not have equal rights. Black people could not drink out of the same water fountains as white people, and some restaurants only welcomed white customers. There were many businesses that wouldn't hire Black people. Vernita moved to Milwaukee, Wisconsin, to find work, leaving Oprah with her grandparents, Hattie Mae and Earlist Lee. Vernita promised Oprah she'd send for her once she was settled.

Oprah's grandparents lived on a farm, and they gave Oprah lots of chores. Besides feeding the animals, she was responsible for going to a nearby well to bring water back for the family. Most of the food Oprah ate was from the farm and garden. She didn't realize that fresh food was a healthy way to eat. Instead she felt ashamed that her family did not have enough money to buy groceries at the store.

By the time Oprah started kindergarten, she already knew how to read and write, because Hattie Mae had taught her how. Oprah was bored watching the other students learn something she already knew how to do, so she took out a piece of paper and wrote the words *elephant* and *hippopotamus*

to show that she could spell and write neatly. She also wrote out names from the Bible. Then she handed her teacher a letter that said, *I know lots of big words. I do not belong here.* The teacher agreed, and with permission from the principal, Oprah was admitted to the first grade.

Oprah lived with her grandmother for the first six years of her life, and then she was sent to Milwaukee to live with her mother. Located along Lake Michigan's shore, Milwaukee was so different from Mississippi. The winters were cold and snowy, and the summers were not as hot. The biggest difference was that Vernita had another daughter by the time Oprah moved in with her. Her name was Patricia. Three people living in a little house, off of a little money, was hard on everyone. After just two years, when Oprah turned eight years old, her mother decided that she should go live with her father, Vernon.

Just as Oprah was getting used to this new way of living in Wisconsin, away from Grandma and the farm, everything was changing again. Oprah was sad to say goodbye to her friends, her sister, her mother. She headed back down South, this time to Tennessee. She didn't take much with her, but she did have her words, her voice.

....

Armed with Faith and Hope

Nothing was the same in Tennessee. Oprah's father had very strict rules: only one hour of television per day, no television on Sundays. He made sure she studied so she would get good grades. Just like when she lived in Mississippi, Oprah recited scriptures at church and the congregation cheered and said, "Amen!" She traveled around town, to other churches in the community, proclaiming the Bible verses that she knew so

well. Oprah became very popular, and that made
some of her churchmates and schoolmates jealous.
Sometimes, on the playground when her classmates

saw her coming, they'd say, "Here comes that preacher girl," and they refused to play with her.

Oprah wasn't bothered by them at all. She knew she wasn't a preacher; she was just a girl who loved words.

She was also a girl who loved playing make-believe with her new friends, Lilly and Betty Jean. They would set up chairs under the maple tree in Oprah's backyard and play *school*. Oprah always played the role of teacher, calling out words for made-up spelling bee competitions.

At church, Oprah learned the Golden Rule: *Do unto others as you would have them do unto you.* She wrote those words down on a piece of paper and kept it in her book bag, keeping it close to remind her to do good. When her church decided to raise money for poor children in Costa Rica,

Oprah started her own campaign at school. She asked her classmates and teachers to donate and give, even if they only had a little. She knew that a little could add up to a whole lot. Living on the farm with her grandmother taught her that. She knew the power of a tiny, tiny seed. How it could grow into being more than enough. How having faith and hope was just like planting seeds in the ground. She believed that if she did good to others, it would come back to her.

But sometimes, it was hard to do good.

At school, there was a girl who was mean to Oprah, so Oprah decided to be mean to her too. Oprah talked about the girl, making it known that they didn't like each other. One day, her friend reminded her of the scripture that she carried in her bag: *Do unto others as you would have them do unto you.* Oprah tried and tried. It was so hard to be nice to someone who wasn't kind. But she believed that if she put kindness into the world, kindness would come back to her, even if it didn't come right away.

At the end of the school year, Oprah went to Milwaukee for the summer to visit Vernita, who had given birth to a son. For the first time, Oprah met her brother, Jeffrey. Now her mother was living in a bigger house, so Vernita, Oprah, Patricia, and Jeffrey had more space. The rules were very different at her mother's house. She could watch television as much as she wanted. Oprah loved watching *The Ed Sullivan Show*, a television program that featured special musical performances. One night, the singer Diana Ross came on the screen. Oprah had never seen a Black woman on television who was so elegant, with diamonds shining around her neck. Oprah was so excited to see a glamorous superstar. "There wasn't anyone on television who looked like me," Oprah said. She would grab a brush and sing into

it like it was a microphone, pretending to sing along with Diana Ross. During those days of pretending and make-believing, Oprah began to dream. She knew that one day she'd be on television too.

Summer came to an end, and Oprah didn't want to go back to her father's rules. She decided to stay in Milwaukee and enrolled in a new school.

Even though Oprah enjoyed fewer rules at Vernita's house, sometimes she was lonely. Her mother spent a lot of time at work. When Oprah was sad or bored, she read books. She also looked after her baby brother, showing him kindness and being the best big sister she could be.

But even with all the good things she was doing, bad things happened to her. When Oprah was nine years old, an older cousin touched her in private places, hurt her body and her heart. She kept it a secret for a very long time. Even though she loved words, some words were just too hard to say, some stories too painful to tell.

....

The Caged Bird Sings of Freedom

Oprah kept her secret tucked deep inside. Vernita had enough to worry about, like not having enough money to take care of her family. Oprah knew her mother was struggling, but neither of them ever said it out loud. But once she turned twelve years old, her mother told her just how bad things were. One winter Vernita took Oprah into a private room, away from Patricia and Jeffery, and said, "We won't be having Christmas this year."

Vernita didn't have enough money to buy gifts. This made Oprah sad and worried about what she would tell her friends. She would have nothing to show them, no special story to tell about how she spent the holiday.

Just before bedtime on Christmas, a group of nuns came to the house with a basket of food and toys for Oprah, Patricia, and Jeffery. Oprah's gift was a Tammy doll. She was overjoyed. She was happy about the doll, but mostly she felt good that people remembered her family existed. Of all the Christmases Oprah celebrated, this one was her favorite. Someone cared, someone showed kindness. That was the best gift to receive.

Oprah decided she wanted to be the kind of person who remembered other people, who did kind things for people in need. She prayed that one

day she'd be able to be a blessing like the nuns who had blessed her.

Until she was able to do more, she continued to give her words.

At school, Oprah's love of reading was noticed by one of her teachers who saw her reading in the cafeteria. He recommended her for Upward Bound, a program that taught important skills that Oprah would need for college. Her teacher had big hopes for her and recommended that she attend Nicolet High School, a mostly white school, far across town in a wealthy part of the city.

When Oprah started at Nicolet High, many people thought this opportunity was a dream come true. But it was hard for Oprah to be excited. When she arrived at school, she realized how different she was from everyone else. Her brown skin was different, the texture of her hair was different, and her clothes were different. For the first time she realized that not everyone lived like she did, that there were some families who had a little and some families who had a lot. Oprah knew her mother was not able to give her any extra money, not even to get a milkshake after school when hanging out with friends.

Even though Oprah was smart and had dreams of being on television and doing good in the world, sometimes she made bad choices. Oprah so desperately wanted to fit in with her classmates, she stole money out of her mother's purse. Once, she ran away from home. Oprah's mother was very disappointed in her. She loved Oprah, but she didn't think her home was the best place for her, so she asked Vernon to come get Oprah, to keep her until she graduated from high school.

When Oprah turned fourteen, she moved back to Tennessee, for good this time. Moving back and forth was hard for Oprah. Friends weren't easy to keep, and her routines kept changing. Being back in Nashville meant she was under Vernon's strict rules and high expectations. Oprah did not want to disappoint him, but she had another secret she didn't know how to tell, and soon she would no longer be able to hide it.

She was pregnant.

The baby boy was born too early and died just a short while after he was born. Oprah didn't tell anyone outside of her family. Another secret buried deep down inside. Some words were just too hard to say, some stories too painful to tell.

Vernon's rules became even more strict. On top of her regular homework, every week he gave her twenty vocabulary words to memorize. He also set a curfew for her and made sure she was not hanging out with friends who would pressure her to do things she shouldn't do. Oprah didn't mind her father's strict rules; they meant she had even more time to read. When she turned sixteen, she discovered the work of author and poet Maya Angelou. In the book *I Know Why the Caged Bird Sings*, Maya Angelou told her story, how she endured abuse when she was a child and how she grew up with her grandmother in the segregated South. Oprah was amazed that someone else had a story like hers, that someone else had the courage to tell stories that were painful. The book became her friend. She read it over and over.

Oprah was inspired by Maya Angelou. If this woman could be so brave, so determined—if this woman could make something of her life and tell her story—maybe, just maybe, Oprah could too.

....

CHAPTER 4

Let Faith Be the Bridge

S ometimes faith is a seed, sometimes faith is a bridge that connects you to your dreams. Oprah started to believe in herself. She focused on school and was a very good student. Her teacher Ms. Haynes traveled with Oprah around the country so Oprah could compete in high school speech tournaments. She also competed in a local pageant, Nashville's Miss Fire Prevention. Winning this honor meant she would visit schools and talk about fire safety. The winner would also receive a wristwatch. Oprah wasn't sure if a girl like her, with brown skin, could win the pageant. So far, only white girls had won.

When Oprah was asked what she wanted her career to be, she said, "I believe in truth . . . so I want to be a journalist and report the news on television."

The judges asked another question. "If given a million dollars, what would you do?" Oprah didn't try to impress them with a fancy answer. She told the judges, "If I had a million dollars . . . I'm not quite sure what I would spend it on, but I would spend, spend, spend!" The audience laughed, and when the winner was announced, it was Oprah who won the crown. She was proud to be the first Black woman to win Miss Fire Prevention.

Oprah had to go to a local radio station to pick

up her prize. The disc jockey, John Heidelberg,
had attended the pageant and was so impressed
with Oprah's presentation that he asked her if she
would like to record her voice in the studio. He
liked the tone of Oprah's voice and thought she

spoke with passion. John gave her a news story, and Oprah read it perfectly on the first take. All those years of speaking at church and in competitions gave her the confidence she needed. It was like she had been reporting the news her whole life. John promised to give the tape to the station manager. The station manager was impressed and hired Oprah.

At sixteen years old, Oprah had a job working at the radio station every day after school and on weekends. Oprah spent the rest of high school speaking at schools and working at the radio station. In 1971, she graduated from high school, making her family proud.

While attending Tennessee State University, Oprah took theater courses and continued to perform around town. The woman with the

confident, passionate voice was invited to audi-
tion to be a newscaster on a local station. In 1973,
Oprah became Nashville's first Black television
anchor. She was also the first woman and the
youngest to ever have this position.

Her dream of being on television had come true. Oprah had just one more course left in college before she would graduate, but she chose to leave college to work at a station in Baltimore, Maryland.

The time had come for Oprah to move away from Vernon. No more back and forth between Tennessee and Wisconsin; this time she was moving out on her own.

Not everything turned out the way Oprah hoped. The station managers in Baltimore thought Oprah showed too much emotion when she was reporting the news. Reporters weren't supposed to cry if the news was sad, or show if they were angry, but Oprah was very honest about how she felt. This was considered unprofessional, and Oprah was switched to doing short reports on the morning news. Oprah was embarrassed and wasn't sure if she could be who they wanted her to be.

But not everything in Baltimore was bad. Baltimore was where Oprah met Gayle King. Oprah and Gayle worked together at the news station. One night, there was a big snowstorm and it was too dangerous for Gayle to drive home. Oprah invited Gayle to stay at her place. There wasn't much sleeping, just a whole lot of talking and talking. They shared stories and got to know each other, and from that night on, they became best friends. Oprah was thankful for this gift of friendship. She wasn't sure how much longer she'd stay in Baltimore, but she knew for sure that wherever she went, she'd remain friends with Gayle.

·····································

Make a Mark on the World

A year later, a new manager started working at the news station, and he didn't mind that Oprah expressed how she felt when she delivered the news. He thought she had an inviting personality, and he promoted her to be a cohost with Richard Sher for a new show called *People Are Talking.* Oprah's job was to interview guests. "This is what I was born to do," Oprah said.

Viewers of *People Are Talking* loved the show so much that the ratings soared to the top of the charts, beating out a very popular show called *The Phil Donahue Show*. For five years, Oprah stayed in Baltimore, but she wanted to do even more.

Her talent with words took her to Chicago to host her very own show, *A.M. Chicago*. This time, there was no cohost to be on-screen with her. The whole show belonged to Oprah. There were people who thought maybe Oprah should stay in Baltimore. They told her how hard it would be. Most talk-show hosts were white men, and most women on television had thin bodies. No one who looked like Oprah had their own television show. And that motivated Oprah even more. She knew there would be challenges, but she knew she had to try. From learning how to read and write at an early age to being the first—and youngest—Black woman to anchor a TV show in Tennessee, Oprah learned how to push herself to be her best, how to never give up.

On January 2, 1984, Oprah's show, *A.M. Chicago*, aired for the first time. Once again, people started watching her show more than they did any other talk show. Her show was doing so well that after just one year the station thought it should be named after her: *The Oprah Winfrey Show*.

The little girl from Mississippi who talked to farm animals to keep company was now talking on television to the whole nation. At times, it seemed like the world was a cruel place, but Oprah didn't let the sadness of her past hold her back. Her light was shining, bright, bright. One day, a music and movie producer, Quincy Jones, was watching

television, and when he heard Oprah's voice, he stopped to pay attention. He was working on turning the novel *The Color Purple* into a movie. As soon as he saw Oprah, he knew she was the perfect person to play the character Sophia.

Oprah's college theater classes and her many years of reciting scriptures at church gave her all the experience she needed to become a good actress. She was so good, she was nominated for an Oscar. Even though she didn't win, she felt special because so many people were cheering her on. Her love of words and belief in her voice had given her many opportunities. That tiny dream to be like Diana Ross was now a big, big dream. She no longer dreamed of being anyone else but herself. She wanted to be the best Oprah she could be. There was so much more she wanted to do.

The Oprah Winfrey Show was seen on more than one hundred television stations in cities across the nation. Oprah soon became a multimillionaire, and now she had an answer for those judges who'd questioned her so long ago at the Miss Fire Prevention pageant. She used her wealth to do good.

Oprah started a production company. She wanted to make movies, not only act in them. Oprah wanted the company to focus on the stories of Black women. She called the company Harpo, her name spelled backward. She purchased a building on the West Side of Chicago, and the space became her headquarters. The building had TV studios, space for filming movies, offices, and even a workout room and cafeteria. Oprah became the first Black woman to own a production studio.

With all these accomplishments, there was still something Oprah wanted to do. She wanted to finish what she started at Tennessee University and get her college degree. She enrolled back in college and finished her courses. On the day of her graduation, she gave a big speech and announced that she was starting a scholarship to honor her father because of his belief in education. The scholarship fund would help students who couldn't afford to pay for their classes.

The more Oprah gave, the more she received. She won many Emmy Awards for her TV show, and she became good friends with the woman who inspired her so much, Maya Angelou. Maya Angelou treated Oprah like a daughter. They shared so much with each other, especially their love of words. And whenever Oprah was

discouraged or worried that she couldn't accom-
plish her dreams, Maya would tell her that she
could do and be anything. She'd remind Oprah,
"You alone are enough. You have nothing to prove
to anybody."

....

Phenomenal Woman

Oprah's talk show became a special hour of television. She not only interviewed famous guests, she shared her own story. The secrets she had been holding in since she was a young girl, she finally told. Sharing her story encouraged others to tell their own. Oprah learned that she was not alone and that the painful things that happened to her were not her fault. She found strength and hope from other people who overcame abuse.

Oprah also used her show to host a national book club. She shared her love of words and encouraged more people to read. So many trusted Oprah's opinion that when she chose a novel for the book club, millions of people would purchase the book and participate.

Reading wasn't Oprah's only passion. She challenged her viewers to donate money to Oprah's Angel Network. It was known as the "World's Largest Piggy Bank." In just one year, the Angel Network raised more than $3.5 million. Because of this money, students were able to attend college and homes were built so that people could have a place to live. Oprah felt so much joy giving gifts. Once, she filled her audience with only teachers and sur-prised them each with a free car. All the teachers cheered.

Even with all her success, Oprah pushed herself to do more. In 2000, she launched O, *the Oprah Magazine*. Her best friend, Gayle, was right by her side. Gayle served as the editor at large and helped to make decisions about each issue.

On a trip to South Africa, Oprah met young people who reminded her of her childhood. There was great need there, and also great talent and passion. Oprah never forgot what it felt like when she was a young girl visited by the nuns who gave her Christmas gifts. Somebody knew she existed. She wanted children in South Africa to have that experience. She created Christmas Kindness and worked with others to give toys, clothes, and food to thousands of children.

Soon after, Oprah founded the Oprah Winfrey Leadership Academy for Girls in South Africa. "When you educate a girl you begin to change the face of a nation," Oprah said.

Oprah also wanted to give back to the place she once called home. She established a Boys and Girls Club in Mississippi. At the ribbon-cutting

ceremony, she told the young people, "You can do
anything that you dream you can do. But you've
gotta do more than dream it. You've got to also

work to make it possible. I come from the same place as you. Anything was possible for me— anything is possible for you."

Anything is possible.

Oprah believed that with her whole heart. It was possible to be teased for loving words and one day become known as the Queen of Talk. It was possible to keep hurtful secrets and one day share the truth and be free of shame. It was possible to start with a tiny light and shine it bright, bright, bright.

After twenty-five years of shining her light on *The Oprah Winfrey Show*, it was time to say goodbye. The last episode aired on May 25, 2011. Oprah held back tears when she told the audience, "You and this show have been the greatest love of my life." Oprah's next adventure was establishing a television network. She called it OWN, the Oprah Winfrey Network. OWN's mission is to create entertainment that inspires and empowers.

To honor all that Oprah accomplished, President Barack Obama awarded her the Presidential Medal of Freedom. The award is given to people who have made outstanding contributions to society. At the ceremony, President Obama said, "Her message was always 'you can.' You can do, and you can be, and you can grow, and it can be better. And she is living proof."

Maya Angelou told Oprah, "Your legacy is every life you've touched."

Oprah told her truth and spoke up for equal rights for girls and women. Even when people said she couldn't do something because she was a girl, or because of the color of her skin, or because of the size of her body, she kept going, kept trying, kept dreaming.

Oprah persisted and you can too.

HOW YOU CAN PERSIST

by Renée Watson

Oprah used her voice to touch people in small and big ways. To honor Oprah's generosity and perseverance, here are some ideas:

1. Memorize a poem and recite it for a loved one. (The chapter titles in this book are all lines from poems by Maya Angelou, who inspired Oprah. If you

are looking for a poem to memorize, one of Maya Angelou's poems might be a great place to start.)

2. Give an unexpected gift to a loved one or friend.

3. Participate in a fundraiser or a campaign to raise awareness about something you care about.

4. Participate in a local community garden.

5. Write a letter to a woman you admire.

6. Start a book club with a group of friends.

Acknowledgments

Thank you to the first women who taught me how to persist. My mother, Carrie Watson, and my sisters Cheryl, Trisa, and Dyan. You all exemplify resilience, grace, and brilliance. Having you to look up to and learn from is such a gift. Thank you to Ellen Hagan and Kori Johnson for reading early drafts and offering feedback. And thank you to my agent, Rosemary Stimola, for offering guidance, always.

Thank you to Chelsea Clinton for your vision and for inviting me into the Persisterhood. To the Philomel team and illustrators: Jill Santopolo, Talia Benamy, Ellice Lee, Alexandra Boiger, and Gillian Flint, it's been a joy and honor to collaborate with you.

If you, or someone you know, need confidential support or need to report abuse, talk to a trusted adult, such as a teacher, guidance counselor, coach, or parent. You can also contact a counselor at Childhelp at 1-800-422-4453.

∽ References ∽

Kelley, Kitty. *Oprah: A Biography*. New York: Three Rivers Press, 2011.

Kramer, Barbara. *Who Is Oprah Winfrey?* New York: Penguin Workshop, 2019.

"Oprah's Boys and Girls Club in Her Hometown." Video. Oprah.com, October 31, 2006.

"Oprah Winfrey Awarded The Medal of
Freedom." The Daily Conversation.
Video, November 20, 2013, https://www.
youtube.com/watch?v=Kp6eGfk1Kn0.

"Oprah Winfrey Biography." Biography.com,
July 30, 2020.

Weatherford, Carole Boston. *Oprah: The Little
Speaker.* Las Vegas: Amazon Children's
Publishing, 2010.

Winfrey, Oprah. Keynote Speech, Variety's
Power of Women Luncheon. 2015.

"Oprah Winfrey's Last Show: Tears and Pride"
ABCNews.com, May 25, 2011.

Winfrey, Oprah. *What I Know For Sure.*
New York: Flatiron Books, 2014.

Winfrey, Oprah. "Oprah Winfrey: Failure
Is the Thing Moving You Forward." View
From The Top Podcast. Stanford Graduate
School of Business, 2014.

RENÉE WATSON is a *New York Times* bestselling author, educator, and activist. Her young adult novel *Piecing Me Together* received a Coretta Scott King Award and Newbery Honor. She is the author of several books for young readers, including the Ryan Hart series: *Ways to Grow Love* and *Ways to Make Sunshine*, *Some Places More Than Others*, and *Harlem's Little Blackbird: The Story of Florence Mills*. Her work has received international recognition and an NAACP Image Award nomination in children's literature. She has given readings and lectures on the role of art in social justice at many renowned places, including the United Nations Headquarters, the Library of Congress, and the US Embassies in Japan, South Korea, and New Zealand. Renée grew up in Portland, Oregon, and splits her time between Portland and New York City.

You can visit Renée Watson online at
reneewatson.net
or follow her on Twitter
@reneewauthor
and on Instagram
@harlemportland

GILLIAN FLINT has worked as a professional illustrator since earning an animation and illustration degree in 2003. Her work has since been published in the UK, USA and Australia. In her spare time, Gillian enjoys reading, spending time with her family and puttering about in the garden on sunny days. She lives in the northwest of England.

You can visit Gillian Flint online at
gillianflint.com
or follow her on Twitter
@GillianFlint
and on Instagram
@gillianflint_illustration

CHELSEA CLINTON is the author of the #1 *New York Times* bestseller *She Persisted: 13 American Women Who Changed the World; She Persisted Around the World: 13 Women Who Changed History; She Persisted in Sports: American Olympians Who Changed the Game; Don't Let Them Disappear: 12 Endangered Species Across the Globe; It's Your World: Get Informed, Get Inspired & Get Going!; Start Now!: You Can Make a Difference;* with Hillary Clinton, *Grandma's Gardens* and *Gutsy Women;* and, with Devi Sridhar, *Governing Global Health: Who Runs the World and Why?* She is also the Vice Chair of the Clinton Foundation, where she works on many initiatives, including those that help empower the next generation of leaders. She lives in New York City with her husband, Marc, their children and their dog, Soren.

You can follow Chelsea Clinton on Twitter
@ChelseaClinton
or on Facebook at
facebook.com/chelseaclinton

ALEXANDRA BOIGER has illustrated nearly twenty picture books, including the She Persisted books by Chelsea Clinton; the popular Tallulah series by Marilyn Singer; and the Max and Marla books, which she also wrote. Originally from Munich, Germany, she now lives outside of San Francisco, California, with her husband, Andrea, daughter, Vanessa, and two cats, Luiso and Winter.

Photo credit: *Vanessa Blasich*

You can visit Alexandra Boiger online at
alexandraboiger.com
or follow her on Instagram
@alexandra_boiger

Don't miss the rest of the books in the

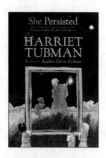

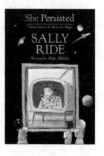

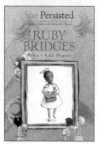

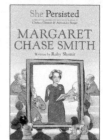

She Persisted series!

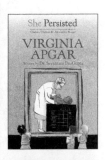

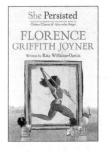

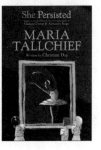

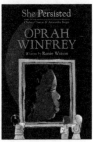